TREVOR WYE

PRACTICE BOOK
for the *flute*

BOOK 1
Tone

NOVELLO PUBLISHING LIMITED
14-15 Berners Street, London W1T 3LJ

HAL•LEONARD®
CORPORATION
7777 W. BLUEMOUND RD. P.O. BOX 13819 MILWAUKEE, WI 53213

FOR MICKY

CONTENTS

	page
Preface	4
TONE EXERCISES—General	5
(a) Harmonics	6
(b) Low Register	7
(c) Middle Register	13
(d) High Register	18
GNOMES	22
TONE COLOUR	24
BREATH CONTROL	27
FLEXIBILITY	27
PITCH CONTROL	34
EXAMPLES	40

A book plus CD version is also available
(Nov 164109)

A PREFACE TO BE READ

TO THE STUDENT

This book is about practising; how to extract the most from it, how to be more efficient at it and how to isolate and overcome some of the difficulties of the flute. It is by no means intended to be definitive. It was written to help you achieve good results with many of the flute problems, in the shortest time.

If the exercises are practised properly, it will shorten the time spent on the building blocks of flute playing, and so allow more time for music making.

These points about practising in general, are important:
(a) Practise the flute only because you *want* to; if you don't want to – don't! It is almost useless to spend your allocated practice time wishing that you weren't practising.
(b) Having *decided* to practise, make it difficult. Like a pest inspector, examine every corner of your tone and technique for flaws and practise to remove them. Only by this method will you improve quickly. After glancing through this book, you will see that many of the exercises are simply a way of looking at the same problem from different angles. You will not find it difficult to invent new ways.
(c) Try always to practise what you *can't* play. Don't indulge in too much self-flattery by playing through what you can already do well.
(d) As many of the exercises are taxing, be sure your posture and hand positions are correct. It is important to consult a good teacher on these points (see page 9 in Practice Book VI—ADVANCED PRACTICE).

GUARANTEE

Possession of this book is no guarantee that you will improve on the flute; there is no magic in the printed paper. But, if you have the desire to play well and put in some reasonable practice, you cannot fail to improve. It is simply a question of *time, patience* and *intelligent work*. The book is designed to avoid unnecessary practice. It is concentrated stuff. *Provided* that you follow the instructions carefully, you should make more than twice the improvement in half the time! *That is the guarantee.*

TO THE TEACHER

This is one of a series of basic exercise books for players of all ages who have been learning from about a year up to and including students at music colleges and universities. There are some recommended speeds, but these should be chosen to accommodate the ability of the player. Some exercises are more difficult than others: take what you feel your students need.

TREVOR WYE 1979

TONE EXERCISES – GENERAL This book is not concerned with any particular school of playing, national style, or with any particular concept of sound production. A good teacher should be your guide. The exercises should be played with your eyes shut; perceptive hearing is thereby enhanced.

Listen carefully *all* the time.
Try not to be distracted by events around you.
If your tone is rudimentary it would be better to start with the low register and build on that.

I have never forgotten the preface to Marcel Moyse' admirable *De la Sonorité*, in which he says, 'It is a question of *time, patience* and *intelligent work*'.

POSSESSION OF THIS BOOK IS NOT ENOUGH.

TONE

When tone is discussed, the word tone is used as a collective noun for a number of desirable qualities, any or each of which contribute a significant part of the overall 'tone'.

For example:
(a) colour
(b) size
(c) projection
(d) intensity
(e) vibrato
(f) purity

If the tone contains desirable quantities of any or all of these ingredients, then it is said to be beautiful. A player's tone is only as good as its weakest aspect. It must be seen that it is impossible to practise any one of these qualities without incorporating others.
Presuming that anyone who takes up a flute and blows it *desires* to produce a pleasant tone, it is difficult *not* to get a sound which, to most ears at least, gives pleasure. The flute head is *made* to give certain tonal qualities which most people would call beautiful.
Therefore, if a student plays long, slow notes to give him opportunity to examine his tone in close detail, then, provided he can *hear* the undesirable aspects of his tone, his self-correcting mechanism will ensure that it improves. Long notes really can't fail to improve your tone!
Nevertheless, long slow notes played without care and thought will not achieve any *real* result quickly. The object of this book is to present a series of steps in tone building, which, if played with intelligence and patience, will achieve the desired result in the shortest time.

HARMONICS

Harmonics, or overtones are the ingredients in sound which give the basic or 'fundamental' tone its colour and character. For the young player, the low and high registers are both difficult but let it be understood that unless the low register tone contains overtones or some richness and colour, the middle and high registers will be the more difficult. Some practice first on overtones will be advantageous.

Ex. 1: Learn to place the notes exactly without them splitting. This is very beneficial.

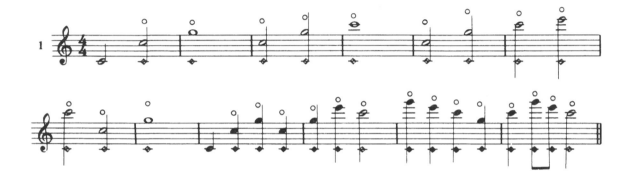

Then try some bugle calls.

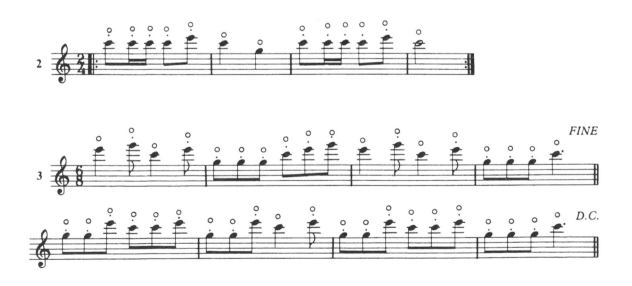

Repeat the three exercises above, fingering (a) low C sharp (b) low D natural (c) low E flat. Notice the increase in air speed required for the higher overtones

THE LOW REGISTER

Whether you begin here or on the later exercises depends on your needs and the advice of your teacher. Assuming that you wish to start by putting the roots of your future tone work firmly in the ground, practise the lower register. But first, you must practise B natural, the easiest note on the flute. It's easy because (a) the shorter the tube the easier the notes are to play and (b) both finger and thumb are holding the flute firmly, a security not so readily available for the two notes above B natural. Play this note – B natural – for as long as it takes to play the best, brightest, most beautiful, rich B natural you've ever played in your life. It *may* take 10-15 minutes. Fine! Unless you have a train to catch, you will achieve more by practising this note than by trying to cover pages of exercises.

Don't play a series of short Bs. Play each B natural for as long as your breath lasts.

When the B natural is really good, commence Exercise 1. Each pair of notes should use up nearly all your air supply; therefore, play them very slowly. Try to ensure that each pair of notes has the *same* quality. Take care not to turn the flute *in* when descending. If the second note happens to sound *better* than the first note, then play each pair backwards.

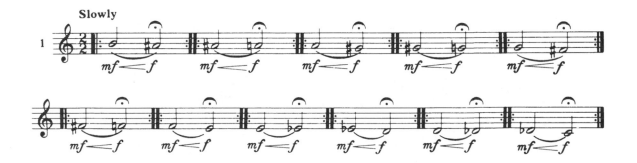

Don't force the tone in the last three bars; it is more difficult to get a good tone here. These last bars may need to be repeated many times.

On your first few days, exercise 1 may well take twenty minutes. Don't worry. There are no prizes for playing the fastest. After several days of practice it is a common complaint that the tone has become worse. This is because your perception of sound is now more acute. Probably your tone *has* improved but having played notes long enough to actually *hear* what is wrong, you are perhaps more aware of your tonal deficiencies.

Now add Exercises 2, 3 and 4 to your practice of No. 1. Remember to repeat each bar just as often as necessary. Not just because it's printed but because you need it!

It is a question of *time*, *patience* and *intelligent work*!

Always start and end your tone practice with a good B natural. It is your reference tone.

*As mentioned before, these last few notes get progressively more difficult. This is because the effective flute tube whilst getting longer does not become wider in bore. If it did, the lower notes would be somewhat easier to play though they would also have a different quality. The tone of the second and third octaves would also be impaired.

You can now add these next three exercises to your repertoire of long notes.
Small adjustments are made to the lips when descending. Take care not to sound like a paper bag full of wasps on your low notes; avoid turning the flute inwards on the lip when descending. Remember to practise the B natural first.

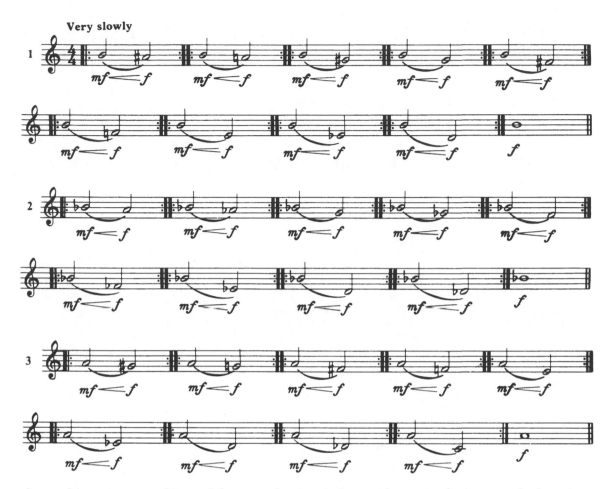

As you become more advanced, here are three more low-register exercises to practise based on:
1) 'The Aquarium' variation from *Carnival of the Animals* by Saint-Saens,
2) a theme from the *Introduction and Allegro* by Ravel, for septet and
3) *Prélude à l'après-midi d'un faune* by Debussy.

1) *The Aquarium* This needs a hollow, 'pure' tone which will be called a 'yellow' tone.*
   Think of deep, dark green water and silent fish swimming gracefully about. Don't forget to practise B natural first followed by C in preparation for this exercise. See also the section 'The Chord of Nature'—Practice Book IV—INTONATION.

*A further explanation of tone colours appears in PROPER FLUTE PLAYING, pp.17-19 (Novello) where these exercises are more fully discussed, and in Practice Book VI – ADVANCED PRACTICE, p.6.

★ (see contents)

2) Ravel§ The Ravel theme needs a somewhat darker, richer tone colour, which we will call 'purple'.

THEME

3) Debussy's *Prélude à l'après-midi d'un faune.*

Here are four low-register exercises based on this well-known theme. Use this exercise to practise a colour somewhere between 'yellow' and 'purple'.

THEME

§*Introduction and Allegro for Septet.* Editions Durand, Paris/United Music Publishers Ltd. By permission.

12

PREPARATION

FINAL EXERCISE

THE MIDDLE REGISTER – I

First, find a good left hand low-register note. It must be your *best* note.

When the note of your choice sounds beautiful, slur up an octave without becoming tense. Don't raise the air stream too high when ascending or the upper note will sound *thin*. Experiment keeping the air stream as low as is practicable in the upper octave and without covering more of the blow-hole. If your upper octave note is not B, slowly ascend to B and practise it for a few moments to make it as bright and as beautiful as possible.

You are going to spread the sound of the B natural downwards into the low register. Therefore, before infecting the low notes, make quite certain that the B natural is a veritable Archangel Gabriel of a B natural before attempting to make the A sharp sound just as good.

As in earlier exercises, play each pair of notes for nearly as long as your breath lasts. Only proceed if the previous pair of notes have been repeated many times to ensure *evenness of quality*. Endeavour also to make the second note even *better* than the first. If this happens at any point, reverse the exercise and work back to B natural which should be even better by this time.

As far as G, all should go well though from G natural to E natural is the first problem patch. Don't force the notes. If these notes sound clear, then proceed. However, for most people, this area from G natural down to E natural has its problems. This is due, once again, to the tube width in relation to its length. This narrowing 'tightens' the notes and causes them sometimes to split. It is during these exercises that you can find out how far you can push a note before it splits. Evenness of tone is what you must strive for.

On descending, if the lower note sounds *better* than the upper one, then reverse the exercise to make the 'reference note' a <u>better</u> reference note!

When some improvement has been made, go back to B natural.

When you reach E flat, there is often a distinct difference in quality. This is the second problem area. Proceed as before, improving the E flat from both the E natural and the D natural.

Ensure that the first finger left hand is raised for E flat and D.*
Raising the first finger for E flat clears this note of its stuffiness. If this area still presents great difficulty, try proceeding by sequential steps.

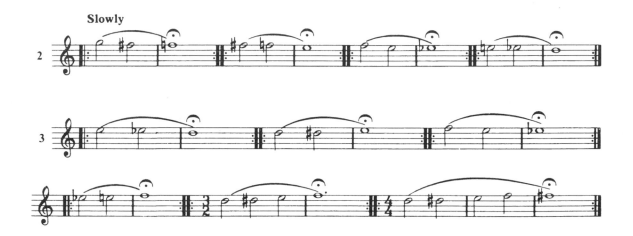

After some days of practice, add Exercise 4 to your daily session. It joins two bars of Exercise 1 together. The tone quality should be the same. Remember to practise the B natural first.

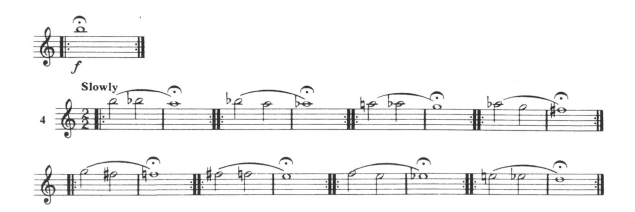

When some success has been gained, add the following two exercises to your repertoire:

*N.B. Exercises for this problem can be found in the companion volumes to this book:
VOL. II – TECHNIQUE and VOL. III – ARTICULATION.

The last bar – above – is there to remind you of problem No. 3: the area around C sharp which is dealt with in the next section. As you descend, the C sharp is the outstandingly empty note. With a different fingering, let us make a *resonant* note out of C sharp, one which, with the *correct* fingering, can be imitated. Whilst descending from D to C sharp, finger C sharp as for *low* C sharp. You must, of course, overblow it. It is full of overtones but it gives one something to grip on. Now try to obtain that same resonance, and *tuning*, with all the fingers off as in the usual fingering. On many flutes, C sharp sounds a little better with the second and third fingers down of the right hand. Try this too, if it helps.

Notice that the C natural sounds better than the C sharp. Check the tuning of both with the overtones* of low C and low C sharp.

Additional exercises to check the tuning and tone of C and C sharp can be found in the section 'Pitch Control' – III. It is useless to practise obtaining C and C sharp with a good tone if the intonation is defective. Get rid of your acne before applying make-up!

Starting with low B, work at the C sharp from this end of the compass.

When some success has been gained, try from both ends.

Then from B natural work your way back up again to the upper B natural..
Remember that each phrase is played *very slowly*.

In Exercise 10, you will try to obtain evenness from middle B natural down to low C
natural. Start off with pairs of notes as in Exercise 1. Then as progress is made, use
Exercises 4, 5, 6 and 10 as your pattern.

You should by now be some way on towards solving the problems of the middle register. Your tone will not improve evenly throughout the range of notes so far studied, though you should now be equipped with enough ideas on how to tackle the difficult areas.
It is a question of_____, _____and_____ _____!

THE MIDDLE REGISTER – II

When both lower and middle registers have been practised for some months, you may find there is still a rather different colour between the lower and middle registers. This exercise will help iron out major differences. Whatever colour you start on, *keep that colour into the middle register*. Practise this exercise first with the 'yellow' aquarium colour, and after, with the Ravel colour, 'purple' (see also PROPER FLUTE PLAYING, p.19).

At this point you will use the colour of the note to help penetrate the leap into the upper note.

PREPARATION FOR

THE HIGH REGISTER

These exercises will help to iron out any change in colour from the middle register to the high register.

They will also help you to 'penetrate' the upper notes – as in the previous section.

Don't raise the air stream too much or your tone will become thin and squeaky.

Endeavour to make the high register sound *noble*.

Top E natural and F sharp are often problem notes. See the section on *Gnomes*.

Using colours in the top register is more difficult, but practise to obtain even a small difference between 'yellow' and 'purple'.

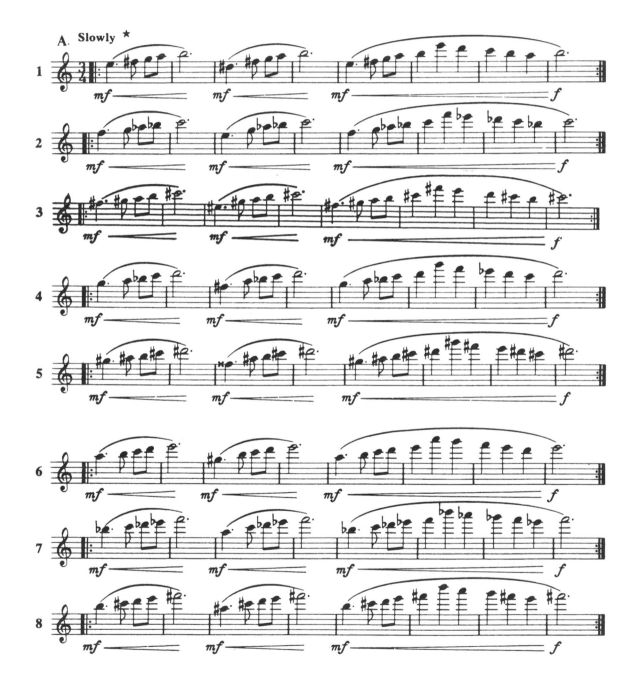

THE HIGH REGISTER

Perhaps these first two octaves have been difficult but the high register is certainly the *most* difficult in which to obtain a good sonority, colour, and depth of tone.

Be sure, before attempting these exhausting exercises, to thoroughly cover the ground in the first two octaves*.

It is better not to practise the high register in the same practice session as the middle and lower registers. Try to do it later in the day.

Remember: it is a question of_____, _____and_____ _____!
You also need understanding neighbours!

See also the next section on Gnomes.

Exercise 1: use the same method of working as for the lower and middle registers. Avoid becoming tense as you ascend.

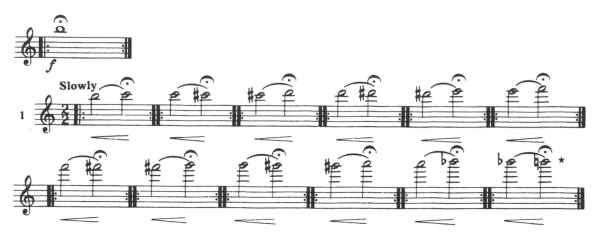

No D sharp key for top B natural

If you wish, go on to high C, C sharp and D, but only if you have the embouchure strength to do this without becoming rigid and tense.

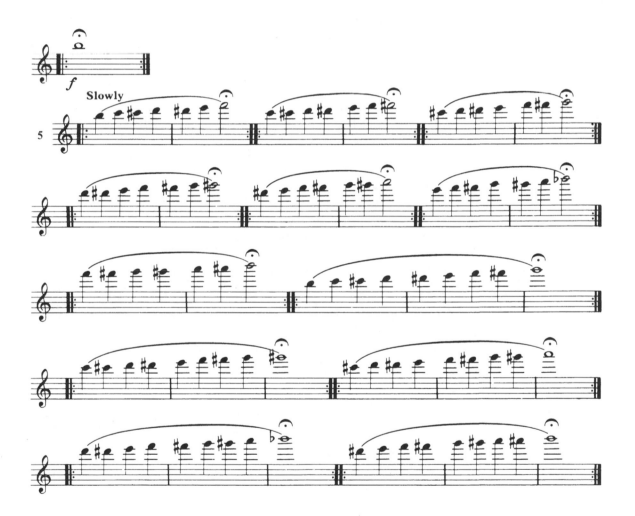

As your work progresses and your lips become stronger, *change the nuances* so as to practise these exercises both *piano* and *forte*.

GNOMES – E natural and F sharp

You may have noticed that top E natural and F sharp are rather sharp. They are also more difficult (without a split E mechanism) than the surrounding notes. There is a mechanical reason for this; if you finger the low register chromatically from low E flat up to B flat, and without blowing, directly compare the fingering with that of the high register, you will see that, apart from E natural and F sharp, there is, in general, one hole open for the comparable upper note. That is, *except* for E natural and F sharp.

Without a split E mechanism, these two notes have *two* holes uncovered with the *comparable* low-register note. If one hole could be closed – as on a split E mechanism flute – top E natural would be easier. A mechanism *has* been invented to close one of the two holes for top F sharp thereby making that easier too. It is called a split F sharp mechanism and is very complex and expensive. It is just another mechanical part which can all too easily go wrong.

With thoughtful practice, I am convinced that neither of these two 'aids' are necessary. With a split E mechanism, indeed the F sharp seems to be more difficult for *psychological* reasons!

Play the scale of G:

The air speed increases when ascending this scale. If difficulty or uncertainty is experienced in obtaining E natural or F sharp then the *air speed* is insufficient to obtain it given that the direction of the air is right. With young players this is a common problem. If, in ascending the scale *piano*, the E natural or F sharp do not sound, then *the notes building up to E natural and F sharp – G, A, B, C and D are the ones to practise.*

If the air speed is not enough to give security to E natural and F sharp then the air speed is probably insufficient to play the *preceding* notes *with proper intensity of sound.*

THINK ABOUT THIS BEFORE PROCEEDING.

In Exercise 1 use more air speed than appears to be necessary to obtain the notes in the first two phrases. No difficulty should then be experienced in bars 6 and 10.

Earlier we discovered that E natural and F sharp are both rather sharp notes. Compare the pitch of them with the harmonics of low C and D.

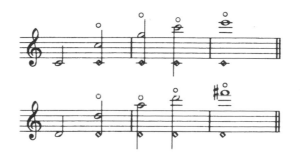

Of course, E natural and F sharp are here being played as fifth harmonics which are 'in tune' but not in accordance with equal temperament!

However, that is another story, and suffice it to say that in the keys of C and D major, try to keep the E natural and F sharp respectively, a little flatter.

Continue with these exercises which demand increasingly more difficult steps. Don't go on until the previous exercise is fairly secure.

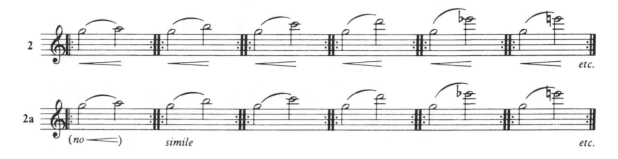

Now try:

If that was too difficult, then try this way around the problem:

Repeat the above but this time with *diminuendo*:

Finally, do Exercise 1 again, but with changed nuances:

Now go back to the top register exercises bearing these points in mind.

TONE COLOUR

The flute is capable of producing a great variety of sounds, more so than any other orchestral instrument. Musical painting is more interesting when the palette has many colours. These exercises will help you to play in 'technicolor' instead of black and white. Play this first exercise A with a full strong, rich, dark 'purple' tone. Try not to turn the head of the flute inwards to do this. It is better to play this exercise loudly.

Tone Colour—Exercise I

Freely = 60-72

after Reichert

Now play Exercise B with a hollow, 'open', gentle 'yellow' tone, more like the recorder in colour. Play more softly than A.

When changing from A to B try to obtain the greatest *difference* in colour. It is the *difference* in tone which is most important.

The most difficult part is to obtain different colours in the *middle* register. *Be sure that the middle register isn't the same colour for both major and minor sequences, even though the low register is different.*

Play through this sequence of exercises in as many keys as you can, but endeavour eventually to play through all twenty-four keys every day as listed at the end of D. It is better to play the exercise from memory; only write out the remaining keys if you *really* have to – it is better to develop your memory skills at this stage.

Then continue in the following sequence of keys: E flat major; C minor; A flat major; F minor *etc.* through a total of twenty-four keys.

Each key has its own colour and its own problems.

After some weeks — and some success — at Exercise I, practise Exercise II in the same way. The intervals in Exercise II are more widely-spaced which makes it the more difficult.

Tone Colour—Exercise II   after Reichert

Remember to make a big difference in tone colour when changing to B.

Then continue in the following sequence of keys: E flat major; C minor; A flat major; F minor *etc.* through a total of twenty-four keys.

Finally, find some books of melodies and practise them using different tone colours. Choose tunes which lend themselves to particular 'colours'. Some examples can be found at the end of this book.

BREATH CONTROL

First consult a good teacher who will put you right about breathing. Otherwise, full explanations with breathing exercises can be found in Practice Book V—BREATHING AND SCALES.

(1) WHISTLE TONES

These are played by blowing the flute in a very *light* and *relaxed* way. They are the notes which sound quietly – and often accidentally – at the end of a diminuendo in the low register. They sound like very quiet squeaks; in fact we often have to practise to avoid them! Try to isolate one of these notes. Finger G natural in the low register to find one of these whistle tones and hold it *for as long as you can* without it 'jumping' or wobbling. Low C natural also produces an easy series of whistle tones. You hardly need any air for these notes. This will help you to control the diaphragm and is equally as good for the lip muscles. A few minutes each day at this exercise will soon show results.

(2) LENGTH

Play middle B natural:

for as long as you can. Check it each day with the second hand of a clock and try to beat your previous day's record. You will soon find ways of exercising economy with the air stream. Within a month you may easily *double* the time for holding this and other notes.

Take care to play the B in tune. It is possible to play a longer note by turning the flute in on the lip and allowing the smaller hole to use less air. Avoid this. It produces a flat, squashed tone and anyway, its cheating!

FLEXIBILITY

To play one note with a good tone is not too difficult and requires the right combination of air speed, air direction, and lip position in relation to the embouchure hole. When moving to another note these ingredients need to change to new values necessary to produce the *second* note with an *equally good tone*. The *changes* and the movements that the lips and air stream have to make from one note to another are what these next exercises are all about. The bigger the interval, the more difficult the changes become. With the right practice you will soon make even large intervals with ease. All the notes should be both beautiful and in tune (*see the exercises on Pitch Control*). Generally the flute sounds louder as it goes up. Do the opposite: practise playing stronger when descending, and softer *but in tune*, when going up. *See preface, note (b)*

FLEXIBILITY—I

after Sousseman

Practise the Flexibility Exercise I firstly like this:

to obtain a good foundation on the low notes, and to check tuning.

Then work up to the G so that it sounds softly, *but not flat*. Try to make the intervals *without strain or undue tension*.

Play the upper notes *softly* and *in tune*.
This may take time.

Then practise the whole exercise in these different ways:

Carefully observe the written nuances. Ask yourself are you playing *really* softly and *really* loudly?

The exercise can be practised in many other ways besides those indicated, including using it as a tone colour exercise.
Tone colour Exercise II can also be used as a *flexibility exercise*.

FLEXIBILITY—II

This is much more difficult and should be attempted only by a more advanced player. The key signature will probably put off less advanced players anyway!

The ways of practising are shown as follows:

Most studies and pieces can be subjected to this kind of practice which is most valuable and beneficial. And interesting!

Some examples from the flute repertoire illustrating flexibility difficulties can be found at the end of the book.

PROBLEMS BOX

1) The exercises are tiring? They certainly are! Be sure to warm up your lips and muscles before practising these exercises. Remember the athlete spends hours warming up before the race or before the practice.
2) Difficulties with intonation? See the *Pitch Control* section.
3) Don't worry about making a lot of movement with jaw/lips initially. Produce a good result *by whatever means* and then reduce the movements without losing what you have gained.

PITCH CONTROL – I

MOBILITY

Playing in tune is inseparable from a beautiful musical performance. This section on pitch control covers the problems of playing loudly and softly, of diminuendos and crescendos without becoming flatter or sharper.

1) Play the C natural fortissimo and at the same time make a diminuendo *without making any corrective movements* with the lips, jaw or head.
The note will go flat.

2) Now play the same C natural, but this time try to *bend* the note both up and down by moving your lips and jaw forward and, if the note won't move enough, also raise your head. *Do not* move your hands, arms or flute to do this.

Before practising loud and soft playing, and diminuendos and crescendos, you will need to obtain enough mobility to enable you to alter the pitch easily and at will. Next, then, practise this jazzy exercise. Do not finger the third note of each bar; make the semitones by bending the pitch downwards.

etc.

PITCH CONTROL—II

NOTE ENDINGS AND NUANCES

It becomes obvious that, as the air speed is reduced (diminuendo) the blow-hole of the flute needs to be correspondingly uncovered in order to remain at the same pitch. These movements of the blowing, together with the lips, jaw and head need to be practised together carefully so as to make perfect diminuendos and crescendos. *Do* count, carefully.

Now try Exercise 2. When you reach the note D *, the pitch is more difficult to 'bend'. Right-hand notes are more difficult to 'bend' than left-hand notes because the tube is longer. The open C sharp is the most moveable note, as we all know, and the most difficult to stabilize.

After several days, or longer, on the first two exercises, go on to Exercise 3, 4, 5 and 6 but don't do the next until the previous exercise is faultless. The reason is plainly clear. The process of co-ordinating both the release of the breath and the lips/jaw/head movement is speeded up until, at Excercise 6 – a 'short ending' – the movement is very quick indeed. This movement should eventually become automatic.

It will be clearly seen that:

(a) there is much to be gained by practising the first three exercises *reversing the nuances;*

(b) it is the method by which the pitch in loud and soft playing, as in 'phrasing' is controlled;

(c) that even loud sustained notes should have a 'short ending' on the end of them.

(d) as you become more proficient, the movement, particularly of the head, will become less.

'SHORT ENDINGS'

Use your new-found technique in Exercises 7 and 8 but be sure to play *really* softly and *really* loudly maintaining the same pitch.

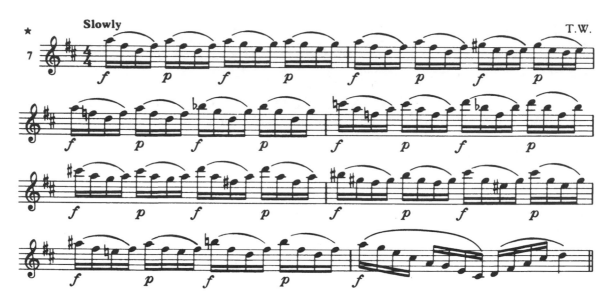

PROBLEMS BOX

1 Never, at this stage, end the notes with your tongue or by shutting your lips together. Use 'endings' to end notes.
2 Don't move the flute inwards or outwards with the hands; use only lips, jaw or head to change the pitch.
3 The end of the note is flat? Move lips, jaw or head more!
4 When the notes get wispy (see Breath Control (I) Whistle tones) push the lips forward more to *stop* them sounding.
5 Check your tuning both before and during practice with a *reliable* piano, tuning fork or tuning meter.

INTONATION*

These exercises will help you control the pitch and tone of both C natural and C sharp and the trill key notes.

First check the pitch of C sharp against the second harmonic, or overtone, of low C sharp. Do the same for C natural.

Then compare the pitch of the upper C sharp with the third harmonic, or overtone, of low F sharp and the fourth harmonic of low C sharp.

Do the same with C natural and F natural.

In Exercises 1 and 1a be sure that the two Cs in the second bar—one harmonic and one natural—are at the same pitch.

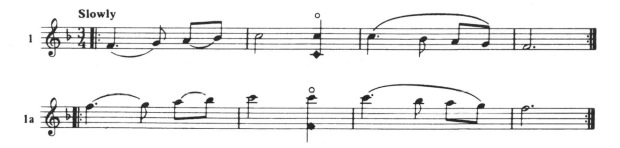

Do the same with Exercises 2 and 2a.

Practise *both* these exercises every day before attempting Exercise 3.

Exercise 3 Here you will make a much quicker comparison between the overtone and the natural note. They must both sound at the *same* pitch.

* A fuller and more detailed study is to be found in Practice Book IV – INTONATION AND VIBRATO.

Exercises 4 and 5 Endeavour to make these rather spineless trill key notes as beefy as the natural notes. It will take a lot of practice but well worth it. Note the fingering:

1 – finger C plus first trill key = D natural
2 – finger C plus second trill key = E flat

Exercises 6 and 7 Play these as though you are using *normal* fingering. Try to be convincing. Note the fingering:

1 – finger C sharp plus 1st trill key = D
2 – finger C sharp plus 2nd trill key = D sharp

Repeat using trill fingerings and normal fingerings alternately.

Exercise 8 Normal fingering is used in this exercise, the point of which is to ensure that C natural and D flat are properly in tune and with a good tone.

Exercise 9 As in the previous exercise. You may find that a flatter C sharp* than in Exercise 8 sounds better in this key, but ensure that E natural is not flattened as well!

If you need more exercises, practise Flexibility I and II.

Some examples from the solo repertoire will be found on page 42. See also Practice Book IV—INTONATION and VIBRATO; the twenty-four studies in that book — one in every key — are invaluable for intonation and phrasing practice.

Finally, remember that the exercises in this book on tone, pitch control and flexibility are all interlinked and dependent on each other. Each must be considered with reference to the others when practising.

The finer points of playing correctly both at equal temperament and to mean-tone tuning will be discussed in Vol. IV—INTONATION and VIBRATO.

EXAMPLES

Here are some extracts from the flute repertoire which illustrate the various points raised in this book.

TONE COLOUR

These are examples where the imaginative flautist will endeavour to capture the intentions of the composer through use of tone colour.

SICILIENNE   FAURE

MADRIGAL   P. GAUBERT[1]

Here, the colours can be changed to suit the keys through which the melody passes.

PAVANE   FAURE

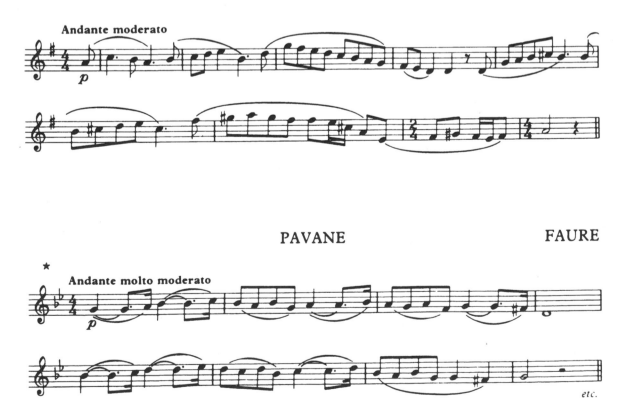

etc.

[1] Reproduced by permission of Enoch et Cie—Paris, UK and Commonwealth agents Edwin Ashdown Ltd.

L'Après-midi is also a good test of breath control. At the very first performance, three flautists were engaged to play the solo in unison because of the breathing problem. Today, it is usual to play it in one breath.

PRÉLUDE À L'APRÈS-MIDI D'UN FAUNE   DEBUSSY

DANSE MACABRE   SAINT-SAENS

SINFONIA FROM CANTATA 156   J. S. BACH

Show the keys by the colour of your tone.

FLEXIBILITY

These extracts show that the wide intervals should be made easily: practice, without undue tension, will give that ease.

PERPETUUM MOBILE   J. STRAUSS

Piccolo

SYMPHONY No. 5   SHOSTAKOVICH

OVERTURE: WILLIAM TELL   ROSSINI

VARIATIONS ON A THEME OF HAYDN   BRAHMS

VARIATION VII

FINALE

SONATE EN CONCERT   J.-M. DAMASE[1]

SICILIENNE

PITCH CONTROL

Note Endings The flute repertoire, both solo and orchestral, abounds with examples of difficult diminuendos whilst striving to stay in tune. Although these pieces are without accompaniment, nevertheless, good intonation is essential. To go flat at the end of any of these works will cause the music to go sour. Check the last few notes with a *reliable* piano.

SYRINX   DEBUSSY

PIÈCE   IBERT[2]

DANSE DE LA CHÈVRE: HONEGGER[3]

[1]Editions Lemoine, Paris/United Music Publishers Ltd. By permission.
[2]Extract from J. Ibert's *Piece for Flute*. Copyright by Alphonse Leduc & Cie Paris. Owners and publishers for all countries.
[3]Copyright Editions Salabert. Used by permission.

A little humour goes a long way and without diminishing the importance of hard, dedicated work, Mr. Wye shows how enjoyable it can be—a most useful addition.

Peter Lloyd

I have read through your book with great interest and believe that it will form an important adjunct to the study and teaching material of the flute. It is just the sort of book which I would have liked to have produced myself. Congratulations on the book and best wishes for its success.

Geoffrey Gilbert

This meets many of the very real problems of the flute in a way not set down in any other book. I shall recommend it to my pupils and shall not hesitate to recommend it to you.

William Bennett

Trevor Wye

Tutors

A Beginner's Book for the Flute   Part 1
       Part 2
       Piano Accompaniment

Practice Books for the Flute

Volume 1   TONE
Volume 2   TECHNIQUE
Volume 3   ARTICULATION
Volume 4   INTONATION AND VIBRATO
Volume 5   BREATHING AND SCALES
Volume 6   ADVANCED PRACTICE

Arrangements for Flute & Piano

A Couperin Album
An Elgar Flute Album
A Fauré Flute Album
A Rameau Album
A Satie Flute Album
A Schumann Flute Album
A Vivaldi Album

A First Latin-American Flute Album
A Second Latin-American Flute Album

Mozart Flute Concerto in G K.313
Mozart Flute Concerto in D K.314 and Andante in C K.315